CORRIE
TEN BOOM

Kjersti Hoff Baez

Illustrated by
Al Bohl

BARBOUR
PUBLISHING, INC.
Uhrichsville, Ohio

Casper looked into the cradle.

CHAPTER 1

The Life of Corrie ten Boom

Casper ten Boom stood looking into the cradle with love brimming over in his heart. It was April 15, 1892, and another little ten Boom had been born into the world. Born prematurely, the baby was tiny and her skin was a bluish color. They named her Cornelia.

The room was filled with aunts and uncles who hovered over the cradle, clucking like hens.

"She'll never make it through the night."

"She's just too weak."

Casper scooped the baby into his arms and shook his head. "She will be just fine," he said. "And we shall call her Corrie."

Cor smiled at her husband and leaned back on her pillows. She whispered a prayer of thanks to God for her newest child. The baby whimpered, and at the sound of her weak little cry, Casper handed Corrie to her mother. Cor wrapper another blanket around the baby and lulled her to sleep.

Between the warmth of the blankets and the love of the ten Boom family, little Corrie grew stronger every day. Betsie, Willem, and Nollie were delighted to have a new sister, and the months flew by.

Like his father before him, Casper ten Boom was a watchmaker. Casper worked in the Dutch city of Amsterdam, but when his father died, they moved to the city of Haarlem so he could take over his father's business. The shop was located on a street called the Barteljorisstraat in an old building called the Beje.

The Beje was a unique house. It was, in fact, a combination of two buildings. The larger building faced the Barteljorisstraat and housed the watch shop and workroom on the first floor. The second and third floors comprised the parlor and five tiny bedrooms. The smaller building in back of this was also three stories high, but its floor levels did not match with the floor levels of the front building. A twisting stairway connected the buildings, making

The Beje was a unique house.

the house seem more like a complicated puzzle than a home.

Life at the Beje settled into a happy routine, with Casper busy in the shop and the rooms upstairs always brimming with people. Cor's three sisters lived at the Beje with the ten Booms. Every morning after breakfast and every evening after dinner, Casper would bring out the old family Bible and read a passage to his family. The Scriptures were as vital to the ten Boom household as food, and their love for Christ spilled over into the lives of all who crossed the threshold of the Beje.

Casper ten Boom worked very hard in his watch shop and eventually became known as the best watchmaker in Holland. His reputation even reached beyond Holland, and it was not uncommon to see young men from other countries come to the Beje to apply for a job as apprentice.

Casper ten Boom was an expert watchmaker.

THE LIFE OF CORRIE TEN BOOM

But it was not his excellent skills as a watch-maker that endeared Mr. ten Boom to the people of Haarlem. His kind and loving spirit was the key to his popularity; the genuine Presence of Christ shone in him. No matter what a person's outward position in society, great or small, young or old. Casper ten Boom loved and accepted everyone.

Casper and Cor prayed earnestly that all their children would serve the Lord. In the midst of cooking and cleaning, Cor ten Boom used every opportunity to bring her children to Christ. When five-year-old Corrie was playing house and visiting the home of an imaginary friend, Corrie's mother told her about a real friend named Jesus who would enter the home of her heart if Corrie would only invite Him in. The little girl with the big blue eyes nodded yes and on the wings of prayer through simple faith, Corrie was born into the kingdom of God.

Corrie prays with her mother.

THE LIFE OF CORRIE TEN BOOM

Corrie and Nollie were close in age, so they often played together in the Beje. One day they paused in their play as the sound of their mother's voice reached their ears.

"Corrie, Nollie!" she called to them from the kitchen. "Are you coming with me to Mrs. Hoog's?"

Mrs. Hoog's baby had died, and Mrs. ten Boom was quick to respond to another's grief. She grabbed her coat and the package of food she had prepared and started for the door. A flurry of footsteps sounded behind her as the two girls followed her out of the house.

Nollie and Corrie volunteered to accompany their mother more out of curiosity than concern. The two girls had never seen anyone dead before, and it was customary to keep the deceased in the home for viewing before the burial.

The girls walked behind their mother, whispering nervously to each other.

The girls hurried after their mother.

"Are you scared?" Corrie asked Nollie.

"Of course not," Nollie responded, knees knocking.

"Me neither," said Corrie, her little hands trembling.

Once inside Mrs. Hoog's, Mrs. ten Boom gathered the young mother in her arms and comforted her without saying a word. Corrie and Nollie stared at the crib with the dead baby in it. Nollie convinced Corrie to touch it, and Corrie was not prepared for the terrible coldness of the baby's skin.

After what seemed like centuries, Momma finally said good-bye to Mrs. Hoog and led her girls out of the door. Corrie and Nollie held their mother's hands and practically dragged her home to the Beje.

Corrie ran up the familiar winding stairway to her bedroom and threw herself upon the bed, weeping.

The sound of her weeping brought her father to her side. Corrie explained between sobs the terror of death and how frightened she was that everyone was going to die.

Corrie ran up the twisting stairway.

Casper spoke reassuringly to his little girl. He told her God was well able to handle our fears if we would trust Him. Even the deepest fear could not separate us from God. In His own way, in His own time, He would take care of all our needs.

"Nothing can separate us from His love, Corrie. That is His promise to us. Not even death can separate us from Him." Casper pulled out his handkerchief and wiped his daughter's tears away.

Corrie looked up into her father's face and gazed at his sparkling blue eyes. She felt completely safe with him nearby. She closed her eyes and listened to the ticking of the many watches that Casper always carried in his vest pockets. For a moment, the little girl sensed that there was something more in her little room than just her earthly father. For a moment, Corrie sensed the unmeasureable love of her heavenly Father surrounding her.

Discovering how wide and high and deep that love truly is would be the adventure of a lifetime.

Casper wiped Corrie's tears away.

It was time to go to school.

CHAPTER 2

At the age of six, it was time for Corrie to start school. The thought of going to a strange, new place terrified her and her young mind searched for ways to avoid the dreadful journey. There must be some way to convince her father and mother that she didn't need to go to school.

Corrie's thoughts were interrupted by the chiming of the clocks in the shop below. The sounds echoed in the halls of the Beje, announcing that it was time for the ten Boom children to go to school. Willem, Betsie, and Nollie bustled out the door, but Corrie didn't move. All the adults in the house tried to explain to the little girl the importance of an education and how she must go to school at once, but it was Casper who eased the child out of the house and down the Barteljorisstraat to the elementary school. Corrie was still scared, but with her father by her side, she knew that somehow she would survive the ordeal.

THE LIFE OF CORRIE TEN BOOM

Corrie did survive her first day and her first year of school. In the years that followed, she enjoyed her studies, but at times she couldn't resist a daydream of a scheme to play a trick on the teacher. Her path crossed with the principal's more than once, and she and her cousin Dot enjoyed many childhood adventures together.

Education continued at home, too. Casper devised games to teach his children other languages. As a result, Corrie learned French, German, and English. Casper and Cor taught their children to love music, and many evenings were spent singing together at the old piano.

Education was very important in the ten Boom household, but it was also important to share what one learned with others. One of Corrie's aunts, Tante Jans, taught the girls to sing hymns to Dutch soldiers that lived in Haarlem. Betsie, Corrie's oldest sister, was a marvelous storyteller, and she taught Corrie how to teach the Bible to children.

The girls sang for the soldiers.

THE LIFE OF CORRIE TEN BOOM

One morning, seventeen-year-old Corrie awoke feeling dizzy. She tried to focus her eyes on the walls of the tiny room she shared with Nollie, but the walls wouldn't stay still and Corrie fell back on her pillow.

"Corrie, are you all right?" Nollie stared at Corrie's ashen face.

Corrie tried to sit up again, but the fever wouldn't let her. The room swirled around her in a dizzying dance. Nollie ran to get Momma. The doctor was summoned and after he left, Casper climbed the stairs to Corrie's room to tell her the doctor's diagnosis. It wasn't going to be easy.

"Well, Pappa, what did he say?" Corrie asked as her father entered the bedroom. She was feeling awfully weak, but surely this was just a case of the flu. Her heart began to pound, however, as Casper looked sadly into his daughter's eyes.

"He says you have tuberculosis." Corrie closed her eyes in terror. She knew the disease was deadly.

The room swirled around her.

Corrie was confined to her bed for several months, and her family prayed faithfully for her every day. It was a struggle for Corrie to accept what had happened; she longed to be out serving the Lord, singing and teaching. But she knew it was useless to argue with God, so she prayed, "Thy will be done, not mine."

The months passed slowly and one day the doctor came to reexamine Corrie. His face lit up with relief as he triumphantly related the news to Corrie and her family.

"Appendicitis, my dear! You don't have tuberculosis, you have appendicitis! I shall operate right away and you will be as good as new!"

Corrie wept for joy and her room filled up with family as everyone gathered around her bed to rejoice over the good news. Corrie knew God's hand was on her life, and He was well able to help her through any trial.

"You will be as good as new!"

THE LIFE OF CORRIE TEN BOOM

The years that followed brought many changes to the Beje. Willem graduated from the University of Leiden and became a minister. He married a girl named Tine van Veen. Nollie chose to be a schoolteacher. Betsie worked in the shop for Casper, taking care of the books and the customers. Corrie helped Tante Anna run the busy household of the Beje.

From 1914 to 1918, World War I rocked Europe, but Holland remained neutral throughout the ordeal. To fight against the fears of those uncertain days, the ten Booms used the best tool they had: prayer. They prayed for all those who were fighting and prayed for the war to end. When the war did end, they put their prayers into action by taking foster children into the Beje. Many people all over Europe were starving for food and compassion. Germany was especially needy, and the ten Boom's foster children were all from Germany.

World War I rocked Europe.

THE LIFE OF CORRIE TEN BOOM

Not long after the war, Momma ten Boom suffered a stroke that made her an invalid. No longer able to speak aloud, she spoke her love through her eyes. Corrie was amazed at the peace that radiated from her mother's face. A paralyzed body could not stop the love inside Mrs. ten Boom from reaching others through that all-important tool — prayer.

Corrie remembered her bout with appendicitis and what a struggle it had been for her to accept being stuck in bed for months. Now, before her eyes, her mother was unable to move or speak, and yet she was still a shining vessel of God's love.

"Dear Momma," Corrie said gently, looking into her mother's sparkling eyes, "How do you do it? How can you be so happy?"

Momma smiled up at her and her eyes seemed to say, "All is well, for I am in the hands of my Lord. He will use me as I am, and in Him I rejoice."

The line from a poem by John Milton traced the air with its truth: "They also serve, who only stand and wait."

Corrie's mother was unable to move or speak.

Willem and Tine lived in the town of Hilversum, and Corrie liked to visit them, especially as their home began to be filled with children. On one visit to see Willem, Corrie met one of Willem's friends from the university. His name was Karel and as Corrie was being introduced, her heart began to pound and her hands started to tremble. She hid her hands behind her back and mumbled a hello.

"Are you all right?" Willem asked his sister. Her face was flushed with color.

Corrie was in love.

From that day on, Corrie and Karel spent as much time together as they could. They talked about everything, and it seemed to Corrie that they were perfect for each other. She was incredibly happy. When she thought of starting her own family with Karel, she could hardly contain herself. Willem, however, did not seem so happy about the new relationship.

Corrie was in love.

Finally, Willem broke the news to Corrie. "H will never marry you, Corrie," Willem said softly "He can't."

"What are you talking about?" Corrie cried ou Fear swept her heart and she became short of breath

Willem explained that Karel's parents wanted hin to marry someone wealthy, someone with a hig position in society. The ten Boom family was definitely poor, and though well loved by the city of Haarlem, they were not high-society people.

Corrie hoped Willem was wrong, but severa months later an announcement arrived from th church Karel was pastoring. It was an engagemen announcement.

The pain in Corrie's heart was unbearable. All sh could picture in her mind was this rich young lad marrying Karel, her Karel. But even as she poure out her grief in sobs, Corrie knew Karel was not her He belonged to the Lord, and Corrie belonged to th Lord, too. His plans for her would never fail, and H knew what was best for Corrie ten Boom.

The engagement announcement arrived.

Corrie busied herself at the Beje and tried no to think of Karel. She prayed often, and as she surrendered her life to the Lord, Corrie's hear filled with peace. She knew whatever the Lord had planned for her would be good and fulfilling.

The day arrived when Nollie was married to a schoolteacher named Flip. She moved out of the Beje into a house on Bos en Hoven Street. Corrie was glad Nollie lived nearby. It was hard to see her go. The Beje was getting to be too quiet. All three aunts had passed away, and the day came when Momma left the Beje, too. Corrie looked around at the empty rooms and was tempted to fall into despair.

Casper laid a reassuring hand on his youngest daughter's shoulder.

"We shall see Momma again. You know that I miss her, too, but Corrie dear, the best is yet to be."

Corrie looked at the empty rooms.

THE LIFE OF CORRIE TEN BOOM

When Betsie became ill, Corrie took over her work in the watch shop. She loved her new job, and the two ten Boom sisters decided to trade jobs. Betsie took over the house and soon had it running smoothly. Following in her mother's footsteps, Betsie was always busy cooking something for someone in need. She decorated the house with color and flowers; she loved her new occupation.

Meanwhile, in the shop, Corrie was making a discovery about herself. She loved the business world. She enjoyed going over the books and dealing with the customers. As she watched her father bent over his workbench repairing a watch with great precision and skill, a desire began to grow within her.

"Father, I want to be a watchmaker."

Casper looked up at her from his bench. In those days it was customary for the son to take up the family trade, but that did not stop Casper and Corrie.

"We will begin your training tomorrow."

"I want to be a watchmaker."

Casper was constantly sharing his faith.

CHAPTER 3

Casper trained Corrie at the shop and then sent her to Switzerland to work in a watch factory. There Corrie learned more about putting watches together. French was the only language spoken there, and Corrie was glad her father had insisted his children learn other languages. She returned to Haarlem and received her license to make watches. Corrie was the first woman in Holland to be a licensed watchmaker.

There was more to life than the watch shop, however. Casper was constantly sharing his faith with everyone he met. He preached the gospel whenever the door was opened to do so and held Bible studies for anyone who was interested. There were always people in the watch shop with Casper, telling him their problems and waiting for his wise counsel. Corrie watched and listened as her father treated each person with the utmost respect, whether they were statesmen or servants.

THE LIFE OF CORRIE TEN BOOM

With Betsie's help, Corrie started a club for young teenage girls. Corrie's faith in God was infectious, and many girls came to Christ through the clubs. There were all kinds of activities and projects, and news of the fun the girls were having spread throughout Haarlem.

Eventually, Corrie started a "Friends" club that included both girls and boys and was a great success. Over the years boys and girls alike enjoyed the fun of the clubs and listened as Corrie and other leaders taught them about the Lord. For many of them, the influence of the clubs would change their lives. They learned that God was near to anyone who called on His name and this wonderful God had a plan for their lives.

Corrie loved working with the teenagers, but there was a Bible school she led that was very dear to her heart, a Bible class for mentally retarded children. The children received the Lord and His Word with sincere hearts. Their intense love and faith in Christ was an encouragement to Corrie's own love and faith.

Corrie's faith was infectious.

Betsie, Corrie, and their father spent the years enjoying the Lord and serving Him. Willem and Tine had four children, and Flip and Nollie had six; the grandchildren added great happiness to their days. Corrie was grateful for the life God had given the ten Booms.

The watch shop had two other permanent workers besides Casper and Corrie. A lady named Toos was the clerk for the shop and an old man named Christoffels worked for Casper as a clock mender.

In 1937, the city of Haarlem joined in the hundredth anniversary of the ten Boom watch shop. It was in 1837 that Casper ten Boom's father first opened up shop on the street called Barteljorisstraat. The Beje was bursting at the seams with people from all walks of life who came to celebrate and 'filled the Beje with affection for Haarlem's "Grand Old Man."

The Beje was bursting at the seams.

The joy of the occasion was dampened, however, when Willem arrived with a young Jewish man from Germany. The man's face was horribly burned. Willem explained that the man had been terrorized by a group of German teenagers.

"I'm afraid this is just the beginning," Willem said, pointing to the man's face. "This is part of the evil that has swallowed Germany whole."

The guests shuddered, but the party continued. It appeared that many in Holland — indeed, in the rest of the free world — had chosen to ignore the alarming symptoms that were surfacing in Germany. There was a powerful man in Germany that very few believed would be of any importance in world history. His name was Adolf Hitler.

The shadows of evening embraced the day and lulled it to sleep. The guests left and the Beje was quiet. Corrie sighed with satisfaction. It had been a wonderful party. But the memory of Willem's guest popped up in her mind and wouldn't leave her alone.

"I'm afraid this is just the beginning."

THE LIFE OF CORRIE TEN BOOM

After the celebration, the routine at the Beje returned to normal. After the daily Scripture reading at 8:30, Christoffels, Toos, and Corrie followed the old watchmaker down the twisting stairs to the workshop. Betsie remained upstairs and cleared the breakfast dishes.

Once inside the shop, Corrie and Toos opened the shutters to let in the morning light. Casper and Christoffels settled down on their workbenches in the workroom. The early rays of the sun rested on the display case and reflected off the gold and silver watches that lay there. Corrie loved this time of day. The sun's light was always brand new. *New every morning,* she thought to herself. *What a perfect picture of God's love — new every morning.*

"Isn't it a gorgeous day, Toos?" Corrie spoke to her fellow worker with great enthusiasm.

Toss only grunted and began to dust the display case.

The watches glistened in the sunlight.

Oh Well, thought Corrie. *It's a beautiful day anyway!* She went back into the workroom to the desk where she handled the bookkeeping for the shop. This never failed to be a source of frustration for her. It wasn't the books that frustrated her; it was the way her father conducted business. Casper ten Boom was definitely not a businessman. A master craftsman, yes; a businessman, no.

Corrie opened the black ledger on her desk and carefully checked the list of sales. Shaking her head in exasperation, she turned to speak to her father. He was bent over his workbench, intently examining the insides of a gold pocket watch from Germany.

"Marvelous! A work of art, that's what it is," he whispered aloud, gently cleaning the tiny wheels and screws of the golden watch.

"Father," Corrie called to him.

"Yes my dear." Casper stopped what he was doing and looked at his daughter. "What is it?"

Casper examined the pocket watch.

"Did you finish the job on the van der Veen watch?"

"Let me see," he mused, tugging on his beard. "You mean the Swiss watch with the engraving on the back? A splendid little machine!"

"Did you finish working on it?" Corrie tried hard not to let her voice betray her impatience.

"Oh yes. Mrs. van der Veen picked it up last Thursday. A lovely lady, Mrs. van der Veen. Did you know her son is studying to be a doctor?"

"Father!" Corrie interrupted what was sure to be a twenty-minute discussion of the van der Veen family. "Did she pay you? What did you charge her?"

Casper smiled at Corrie, his eyes as true blue as when he was born seventy-nine years before. "Corrie, how could I charge her? That watch is an antique, you know, and has been in the van der Veen family for many, many years." He cleared his throat with enthusiasm. "It first belonged to Hans van der Veen and he. . . ."

"Did she pay you?"

"Oh Father!" Corrie cut him off with a groan. "Did you at least give her a bill?"

Casper laughed and returned to his work. "What a worrywart you are, my dear!"

Corrie sighed and turned back to her books. *It's a wonder we haven't gone bankrupt,* she thought to herself. *Sometimes I think he's too generous.*

And yet she knew they always managed to do more than just make ends meet. Yes, there were some who took advantage of Casper's generosity, but many of their customers did pay their bills, and things had a way of working out. From Momma's stove to Poppa's workbench, the ten Booms were known as a giving family. Momma's love and soups had comforted many a weary soul, and the watchmaker's wise counsel helped repair many a broken heart. This was not because the ten Booms were givers by nature, but because the greatest Giver of all lived in their hearts and home.

From stove to workbench,
the ten Booms were givers.

" Willem! "

CHAPTER 4

The doorbell in the alley jangled impatiently, and Corrie hurried to the hall behind the workshop to open the door. A delivery boy handed Corrie a pile of packages and tipped his hat. She reached into her dress pocket for the tip but to her surprise, a hand reached out from behind her and paid the boy.

Corrie swung around and was immediately surrounded by two strong arms.

"Willem!" She laughed and kissed his bearded face. "What are you doing here?"

Placing his hands on her shoulders, he gently directed her toward the shop. "Back to work, little sister."

Corrie laughed. "Little sister, indeed! At forty-five years of age, I'm not exactly a schoolgirl!"

Corrie's laughter reached the workshop before she did and Casper looked up from his workbench.

"I see you've run into your brother, Corrie!" Casper's eyes twinkled behind his wire-rimmed glasses as he surveyed his two children. Corrie placed the pile of packages on her desk.

"Yes, Father. He's teasing me as usual, and. . . ."
She stopped in mid-sentence. All of the packages
were stamped with a message in bold red letters:
"Return to Sender."

"Why, these are all the packages we sent to
Germany this month. I don't understand it.
We've done business with these suppliers for
years! I wonder what in the world. . . ." Her voice
trailed off and she sighed. Another frustration to
be faced. German watches were among the finest
watches in Europe, and the ten Boom shop sold
many of them in the course of a year.

"Let me see the packages, Corrie." Willem's
tone was strangely serious. He picked up the
packages, glancing at the addresses on each one.

"What do you notice about the names on these
boxes, Corrie?" he asked sternly.

Suddenly, Corrie felt like a little schoolgirl
again, being questioned by her older brother. She
looked at the addresses, but nothing clicked.
Willem's tone of voice disturbed her and she was
unable to think straight.

Willem picked up the packages.

"I don't know, Will, I can't tell. . . ."

"Read the names! The names!" Willem's anger exploded in the air and Corrie stared at him, shocked. All eyes were on Willem. Even Toos ran in from the shop to see what was the matter. Casper ten Boom's voice penetrated the bizarre scenario.

"What is the meaning of this, my son? What are you trying to say?"

The sound of his father's voice settled onto Willem's anger like snow on a fire and as quickly as the anger had come, it flickered out. Willem reached over and took Corrie by the hand.

"I'm sorry, my dear Corrie. It's just that. . . ." He stopped and pointed to the names on the packages. "Look — Kaufman, Rubenstein, Lieberman — don't you see?"

"Why, those are all Jewish names, Willem." Casper looked at his son with questioning eyes.

"Yes, Father. All Jewish."

"But I still don't understand." Corrie stammered.

All eyes were on Willem.

"The Nazi movement in Germany is no longer just a terrible idea. The German leaders are putting into practice what Adolf Hitler has hammered into their heads. The Jews are considered to be subhuman enemies of the German nation. All over Germany, Jews are disappearing."

Corrie and Casper looked at each other, not wanting to believe what they were hearing. But deep inside they knew Willem was right. Ten years before, while studying for his doctorate in Germany, Willem wrote a paper warning people of a dark way of thinking that was quietly invading the German universities. No one believed him then, but now it was all too real.

Willem cleared his throat and made a feeble attempt to sound cheerful.

"Our nursing home in Hilversum is overflowing now with Jewish refugees. With God's help we will be able to take care of them until this madness ends."

"All over Germany, Jews are disappearing."

If we can be of any help, my son, let us know." Casper sat down at his workbench and resumed his study of the German watch. The laughter that had filled the air only moments before was gone now. In its place there hung a heavy sadness.

Corrie slipped her hand around Willem's arm. "Won't you stay and have lunch with us?"

"No. Thank you, but I really must be getting back to Hilversum. Tine's got her hands full as it is." He kissed Corrie on the cheek, bade his father good-bye, and was gone.

With a sigh, Corrie returned to her desk and gathered up the packages. Now the bright red letters glared up at her, symbols of evil. She hastily unwrapped each one and threw the papers in the wastebasket.

The red letters glared at Corrie.

The next two years were fairly normal at tl
Beje. Elsewhere on the European continer
however, things were far from normal. Under tl
leadership of Adolf Hitler, Germany seiz
Austria and Czechoslovakia and then set i
hungry eyes on the country of Poland. This w
sure to spark the outbreak of World War II, ar
Holland hoped it would maintain the neutr
status it held in World War I. Surely the ugly te
tacles of war would not reach over and cross tl
borders of fair Holland!

In the front room of the ten Boom watch sho
the bell on the door rang loudly as a young mi
strode into the shop.

"I wish to speak with Mr. Casper ten Boom
He spoke abruptly, looking at Toos impatientl
"Go get him," he commanded.

"And who are you?" Toos asked, ice in h
voice. She was not easily flustered, and she too
commands from no one except her employer.

"I wish to speak with Mr. ten Boom."

The man turned his back on Toos and heade
for the workroom, "I'll find him myself."

"You can't go back there!" Toos shoute
after him. "Who do you think you are?" Sh
quickly followed after him, her face red wit
anger. The young man burst into the workroom
At the sight of Mr. ten Boom, he stopped an
bowed graciously.

"Mr. ten Boom. My name is Otto Altschuler.
am from Berlin and wish to be your apprentice.'

Toos stood behind him, glaring.

"He just barged right in, Casper, and didn'
even wait for me to get you. Of all the rude, in
considerate. . . ."

"Now dear Toos, thank you for showing Mi
Altschuler in. I think I hear the front bell ringin
again."

At Casper's gentle prompting, Toos turned o
her heel with a huff and stomped back into th
watch shop.

"My name is Otto Altschuler. "

"Allow me to introduce my associates," Casper continued. "This is my daughter Corrie. She was the first woman in Holland to become a licensed watchmaker." He beamed with pride. "And this is Christoffels, my highly skilled clock mender." Otto barely nodded at Corrie, and he totally ignored Christoffels.

"Here are my papers, sir. I have come with excellent references, as you can see."

Casper scanned the papers quickly and nodded in agreement.

"These are excellent recommendations. You can begin work tomorrow. You are welcome to join us at 8:30 for coffee and Bible reading." He shook the young German's hand.

"Thank you, sir." He bowed respectfully and then left as quickly as he came.

Much to Corrie's relief, the rest of the day ran smoothly. The January sun retired early, its golden light lingering for a moment over the Barteljorisstraat. The watch shop was empty as Corrie gazed out

Otto left as quickly as he came.

the front window to savor the last of the day's sunlight. When the sun's rays retreated altogether, she closed the shutters.

Otto was a fast learner, and Casper was delighted with the young man's progress. There was, however, a threatening thread that wove its way through the shop whenever Otto was there. He refused to join the ten Booms for the Bible reading, and although respectful of Mr. ten Boom, Otto treated Christoffels shamefully. Whenever he had the chance (whenever Casper was not in the room), Otto would taunt Christoffels and call him a "worthless old man."

Weeks later, the secretive evil reared its head in full view of the ten Boom family. On a cold winter morning in 1939, just as Casper opened his Bible, shouts rang out in the alleyway. Corrie and Betsie rushed to the alley door and found Christoffels, his face covered with blood.

Mr. Weil, the furrier who lived across the street, handed Corrie the old man's hat. Betsie helped Christoffels up the stairs into the Beje.

Christoffel's face was covered with blood.

"Christoffels! What happened?" Casper hurried over to his colleague.

"It was that apprentice of yours, Casper," Mr. Weil explained. "He pushed the old man into the wall and held him there with all his strength." The furrier's voice boiled over with anger. "It's an outrage! It's not the first time I've seen such goings on! You'd better do something about it, my friend."

Stunned, Casper turned to Christoffels. "Why didn't you tell me this was happening?"

Christoffels said nothing. He was too proud to ask for help from those who loved him best. Casper's heart broke as he thought of the old man being terrorized for weeks by the young German.

"Can you forgive me for being so blind? I had no idea. . . ." Casper's voice trailed into a tense silence. He left the old man to Betsie's tender care and descended the stairs to the workshop. Corrie followed after him, sensing anger in the air.

Casper hurried over to his colleague.

THE LIFE OF CORRIE TEN BOOM

They found Otto at his workbench, already busily repairing a Swiss wristwatch. He greeted his employer and resumed his work. Casper put a hand on the young man's shoulder.

"I'm sorry, but you must leave us. There is an old man in my home with blood on his face and terror in his eyes because of you. Surely you must know that the dark road you are traveling leads only to a greater darkness. Turn around, my son, before it is too late."

Corrie trembled in anticipation of an explosion, but Otto was silent. He slammed the door as he left, and father and daughter stood alone in the shop, numb with shock. This was their first face-to-face encounter with the black heart of the Nazi movement.

Corrie hoped it would be their last.

Otto slammed the door.

Corrie gazed at the radio.

CHAPTER 5

In the spring of 1940, the shadow Adolf Hitler cast over the face of Europe grew deeper and spread itself north to Scandinavia. In April, the German army began its invasion of Norway, seizing the country of Denmark. The little country of Holland still clung to the hope that its neutrality would be honored. On the evening of May 9, people all over Holland gathered around their radios to hear what their prime minister had to say about the fate of their country. Fear of war curled its cold fingers around the hearts of the people.

In the parlor of the Beje, Casper ten Boom and his two daughters waited for the prime minister to speak. Corrie gazed at the radio, remembering evenings long ago when the ten Boom family and friends would gather in the parlor to listen to breathtaking Bach or Beethoven. But Corrie knew tonight there would be no music.

When at last the prime minister's voice crossed the airways, his message was one of peace. Holland would not be invaded, but would remain neutral. Betsie and Corrie looked at each other and sighed with relief, but Casper scoffed at the prime minister's words.

"Holland will be invaded," he said. "There is no use denying it."

Casper's words echoed over and over in Corrie's mind as she tossed and turned in her bed that night.

Several hours later, in the cold darkness of the predawn air, German soldiers swiftly and silently parachuted onto Dutch soil near Rotterdam and The Hague. With the help of Dutch Nazi sympathizers, they captured strategic bridges and attacked the nation's airports. At dawn, the Germans launched a ground attack on southern Holland, successfully gaining control of the railroad bridge that spanned the Maas River. Their invasion was complete; they had Holland pinned to the wall.

*German soldiers swiftly parachuted
onto Dutch soil.*

The sound of an explosion ripped through the air and jolted the city of Haarlem out of its sleep. Betsie and Corrie prayed together, simultaneously, urging the ears of heaven to hear their cry and help; save the country. Corrie finally fell silent. She could only weep quietly for her country and her people.

Suddenly before her eyes there passed a vision as clear as a picture on a wall. Corrie saw a wagon drawn by four black horses in the town square. The wagon was filled with people she knew. She saw Father, Willem, her nephew Peter, Toos, and other friends of the family, all seated in the wagon. Betsie was there, and Corrie sat there also. The horses were taking them somewhere strange and terrifying, but they were helpless to do anything about it.

The vision faded. With a trembling voice, she related the story to Betsie.

Four black horses pulled the wagon.

Four days later, on May 14, the Germans gave the Dutch an ultimatum: If they did not surrender within twenty-four hours, the Germans would bomb Rotterdam and Utrecht. The Dutch continued to fight, and two hours before the ultimatum was up, the German air force totally destroyed the business section of Rotterdam. The number of civilians whose lives were devastated by the bombing were horrifying: There were thousands of casualties. Unable to resist the ruthless invader any longer, Holland surrendered.

News of the surrender sent shock waves throughout all of Holland. The unthinkable had become reality. Germany had conquered, and Germany would rule. Immediately, the effects of the new government were felt by the Dutch. No one was allowed on the streets at night after 10:00 P.M. In order to make purchases in any store, a person had to use ration cards instead of money. Everyone was forced to wear identification cards.

Holland surrendered.

THE LIFE OF CORRIE TEN BOOM

The city of Haarlem watched silently as the Germans marched down its streets to take control. Corrie pulled back the curtain in the shop window and looked up and down the Barteljorisstraat. The street was swarming with soldiers.

"It's like a dream," Corrie whispered. "I can hardly believe what I am seeing."

"It is a nightmare," Toos replied quietly from behind the display case. "It is as if evil is taking over the earth."

Corrie looked at Toos with surprise. The stern old clerk rarely shared her feelings with anyone. Corrie crossed the room and took the old lady by the hand.

"God will see us through this, Toos. No matter what happens, He will be with us."

Toos nodded wordlessly, tears streaming down her face. She retrieved a handkershief from her pocket, wiped her face, and cleared her throat. "And now, Miss ten Boom," she said formally, "as Casper would say, 'Time for work!' "

The street was swarming with soldiers.

Corrie walked back to the workshop to find Nollie's teenaged son Peter perched on his grandfather's workbench. His face was flushed with anger, and he was speaking loudly to Casper.

"So now what, Grandfather? They are demanding that everyong bring their radios to the department store. What are we going to do about that?"

"Peter, I'm not deaf, yet. Slow down and tell me again — in a normal voice this time." He smiled at his earnest grandson, and Peter made an effort to calm himself.

"What are you talking about, Peter?" Corrie asked. "What's that you said about the radios?"

"The Germans want every Dutchman to bring his radio to the department store downtown. No one will be allowed to have a radio in their home. And I also heard that all telephones will be disconnected. How do you like that?"

" What are we going to do? "

"They're trying to cut our throats," Peter con
tinued. "We'll be helpless without any way to
communicate freely. And I suppose everyone will
follow orders, just like a bunch of sheep." He was
speaking loudly again, unable to control his
anger. Casper put his arm around his troubled
grandson.

"First of all, Peter, you must understand that
the Germans are in control now. There is not
much we can do about that. Your anger is justi
fied, but you must not let it control you. You've
got a good head on your shoulders, Peter. Don't
let it be ruled by how you feel. If we are to help
our country, we must be able to think clearly."

"Yes, Grandfather." Peter got up from the
bench and headed for the stairs. "Guess I'll get
something to eat," he mumbled. Corrie's heart
went out to him as she listened to him climb the
stairs, dragging his feet. Midway up the stairs, the
sound of Peter's labored steps ceased on the
stairwell.

" We'll be helpless! "

Corrie started for the door to see what was the matter and was almost knocked over by her nephew as he raced back into the workshop.

"I've got it! I've got it!" He shouted excitedly at Casper. "It's perfect!"

"What on earth are you talking about, Peter? And please, my ears!"

Peter took a deep breath. "I know what to do about the radio! You've got two, don't you?"

"Well, yes. There's the large one in the parlor and the small one Pickwick gave us in the kitchen."

"Right. So, we only turn in one of them!"

"And what, pray tell, do we do with the one we keep?" Corrie asked, shaking her head. "We can't just keep a radio in the house. The Germans are known for their unexpected visits. The radio would have to be invisible!"

"Precisely!" Peter smiled broadly. "Invisible."

"I give up. What are you up to now?" Corrie sat down at her desk and waited for her nephew to explain.

"I know what to do!"

"We will hide the big radio in one of the steps of the stairwell. Those winding old steps are perfect. They'll never find it."

Corrie looked at her father, expecting to see him disapprove of such a plan. Instead, she saw him smile and slap Peter on the back.

"Now that's using your head!" He laughed, picking up the watch he had been working on. "Time for work."

Peter walked back to the stairs and echoed his grandfather's words. "Time for work."

In less than an hour, the secret step was finished. Peter placed the big radio in its new home and grinned in triumph. Corrie and Betsie marveled at Peter's job. Neither of them could tell which step had been tampered with.

"What do you think?" Peter asked his aunts.

"It's fantastic, Peter! You're really quite a wonder!" Betsie gave him a gentle hug.

"Invisible," Corrie replied. "Absolutely invisible!"

The winding steps were perfect.

"Thank you, thank you." Peter bowed dramatically. "And now, Tante Corrie, it's up to you to carry out the rest of the plan. You must go downtown and turn in the other radio. Remember, it is the only one the ten Booms own." He held her gaze with his serious eyes and she understood what he was saying to her. Those in charge of collecting the radios would surely ask if this was the only one in the house. Corrie would have to lie.

Several hours later, her mission accomplished, Corrie made her way back to the Beje. Questions flooded her mind. When a nation is captured and treated cruelly by another nation, what is right and what is wrong? Corrie wondered what her dear mother would say if she were alive now. Secret steps, hidden radios, and deception — these things were all foreign to Corrie, and yet they seemed necessary in this time of great darkness.

Betsie greeted Corrie at the door in the alley and ushered her into the dining room. She handed

Mission accomplished.

her younger sister a cup of hot tea. Seeing th
troubled look on Corrie's face, Betsie sought t
comfort her.

"We can only do our best, Corrie. The Lor
expects nothing more than that. We can only pra
that we will have His wisdom in these hard day:
He will guide our steps."

Corrie smiled wearily and sipped the hot te;
She watched as Betsie busied herself with the po
on the stove. *I wish I had your strength,* Corr:
thought to herself.

"He will guide our steps."

Holland was gray with hunger.

CHAPTER 6

The days hurried into months, and the Germans tightened their grip on the Dutch people. The curfew was constantly being changed to an earlier hour until it was almost impossible to go out in the evening. With the approach of winter, food supplies diminished. Meat was rarely available; coffee and tea were unheard-of luxuries. Holland was gray with hunger of body and soul. They looked on with anger and sorrow as many fellow Dutchmen turned their backs on their heritage and joined the National Socialist Bond, the Nazi organization of Holland. Holding out the promise of more food and clothing, the NSB grew in number. The Nazis brought with them their hatred for the Jews, and soon its poison took effect on the streets of Haarlem.

Corrie closed the door in the alley and joined her father on the Barteljorisstraat. Slipping her arm through his, they walked slowly down the narrow street, the bright September sun gently warm upon their faces.

They chatted and shared memories as they continued down the Barteljorisstraat, unaware for a moment that their afternoon walks would never be the same again. Casper noticed it first.

"What in the world is that, Corrie?" She looked as he pointed to a young couple crossing the street.

"I don't see what you mean, Father. What are you. . . ." She tried to get a good look at the man and woman without appearing rude. There was something different, but what was it?

"What's that they're wearing?" Father whispered. "On their coats. A yellow star."

"Yes. I see it now. And look — that man over there — he's got one, too." Corrie and Casper stopped for a moment, bewildered.

"I'll ask Mr. Weil. He'll know," Casper said, turning around. He started walking again, at a quicker pace, and Corrie hurried beside him.

Casper noticed the yellow stars

Mr. Weil was standing in front of his fur shop, briskly washing the window. The cleaning cloth in his hand was a blur of white as he rubbed the window in furious circles.

"Excuse me, Mr. Weil," Casper began, "I was wondering. . . ."

Mr. Weil spun around to face them, and the star on his coat jumped out at them in a flash of yellow. In big black letters the word "Jew" screamed its presence in the center of the star. Father and daughter tried to speak, but no words would come.

"Ah ten Boom, it's only you," Mr. Weil spoke with relief. "I thought maybe — well, never mind. Did you want something? What's the matter? You two look as if you've had quite a shock." His large dark eyes searched their faces, then he realized they were staring at his coat.

"Oh, so that's it." He pointed to the yellow emblem.

Mr. Weil spun around to face them.

Mr. Weil pointed to the yellow emblem. "This is the latest in fashion from the Nazi regime." His voice was strained with artificial humor. "Of course it was designed exclusively for those who are Jewish." His sarcasm marked his pain, but Casper was not fooled. He took Mr. Weil's hand and held it a long time, saying with his eyes all that could not be said with words. Corrie stood silently by, her vision blurred as tears filled her eyes. *Dear God. What does all this mean?*

"I really must be getting back to work."

Casper tipped his hat to the furrier and took his daughter gently by the arm to cross the street. Casper entered the watch shop and Corrie closed the door carefully, wishing that by closing the door to the street she could close out the heartache of the day. But Corrie knew that was impossible. As she sat at her desk, the strange yellow star would hang in her mind like an unwanted flag.

"What does all this mean?"

Several months later, the sound of marching men echoed through the Barteljorisstraat. Corrie looked out the front window of the shop and watched as a group of German soldiers broke into Mr. Weil's shop. They shoved Mr. Weil out of his store and proceeded to destroy the place.

Corrie's heart pounded as she quickly ran out the door and headed for Mr. Weil. She heard footsteps behind her, and in a flash Betsie was at her side. Together they grabbed Mr. Weil and rushed him into the Beje. Casper joined the frightened trio in the dining room and spoke kindly to his neighbor.

"You are safe here with us, my friend. God will tell us what to do."

Mr. Weil looked up at Casper with fear in his eyes.

Corrie felt her heart begin to race. Suddenly the answer flew through her spirit like a swift, silent arrow.

The soldiers broke into the fur shop.

"Willem will know what to do." She spoke the words with such confidence that she startled everyone.

Corrie left at once for Willem's home. Willem's son Kik answered Corrie's knock and ushered her into the kitchen where Tine was busy preparing lunch. Corrie greeted her sister-in-law with a hug and plunged into her story. Kik and Tine listened carefully but didn't seem to be at all shocked as Corrie related her hair-raising account of Mr. Weil and the soldiers.

"And so you see, I must speak with Willem right away," Corrie finished excitedly. She looked at Kik and Tine and wondered how they could remain so calm.

"Willem is not here right now," Tine replied, wiping the kitchen table with a soft blue rag. "Kik will take care of it for you."

Corrie stared in amazement at her tall young nephew.

"Kik will take care of it."

"But what could you. . . ." Corrie started to protest, but Kik wrapped an arm around his flustered aunt.

"Don't you worry about a thing, Tante Corrie. You just listen to my directions and do exactly as I say. I will knock on the door in the alley tonight," Kik explained. "Before you open the door, make sure the hall light is off." He turned to his mother. "When Dad gets back, tell him I might not get back until tomorrow afternoon." Kik kissed his mother and Corrie good-bye and was gone.

"What's the matter, Corrie?" Tine stopped her work for a moment and sat down at the table. "Kik is not a little boy any more."

"But he's so young. How does he know what to do? His plan came to him so easily you'd think he'd done this kind of thing many times before."

Tine said nothing but looked steadily at Corrie. Suddenly Corrie realized what Tine's silence meant. Kik, Tine, Willem — they were all

"Do exactly as I say."

involved in the work of the Dutch underground! This illegal group of brave men and women did its best to sabotage the Nazi regime in Holland and help those who were special targets of the German army.

Corrie started to ask Tine a question, but Tine stopped her.

"The less you know, the better, Corrie. That is the policy of the underground movement. That way, if anyone is caught, they will not reveal any information the Gestapo is looking for. They can't stop us if they don't have any names to go on."

Tine patted Corrie's hand. "I think you'd better get back to the Beje. Mr. Weil must be ready to leave at nightfall."

As Corrie traveled back to Haarlem, she realized a plan was beginning to unfold. Corrie, Betsie, and Casper had crossed the line and entered into the underground simply by arranging things for Mr. Weil's safety. She sensed it was the Lord's plan and there was no turning back.

"The less you know, the better."

When the evening finally came and draped its darkness around the city of Haarlem, the ten Booms welcomed its covering. A knock on the alley door signaled Kik's arrival, and the ten Booms gave him the precious life they had been sheltering there all day. Kik took Mr. Weil gently by the arm, and in a moment they were gone. Casper, Corrie, and Betsie stood in the darkened hall for a long time, praying that all would go well. They were now a link in the underground, and in the days to come, God's plan for saving lives would unfold before them in a tapestry of intrigue and danger.

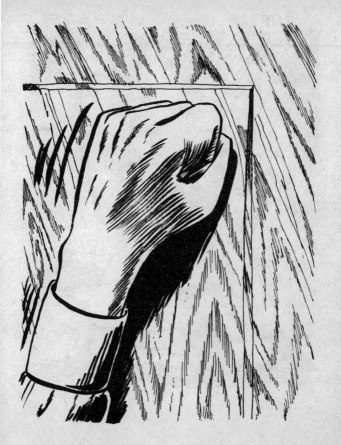

A knock on the door signaled Kik's arrival.

The soldiers seized men without warning.

CHAPTER 7

In 1942, spring slipped into place without the usual stirrings of hope and new life. The Nazi leaders in Holland did their best to break the spirit of the people. More and more, the Dutch felt like caged animals. Curfew was now set at 8:00 P.M. It was no longer safe for young men to walk the streets during the day because Germany needed manpower for their ammunition factories. Without warning, soldiers would seize men on the streets and ship them off to Germany to work for the Nazis.

The word spread among the Jews of Haarlem that the ten Boom family on the Barteljorisstraat had helped a Jewish furrier escape from the Nazis. In a matter of weeks, young mothers with children, elderly couples, and middle-aged men appeared at the alley door of the Beje. All were desperate for shelter from the searching eyes of the Gestapo.

With help from Willem and his friends, Corrie organized the underground operation at the Beje. The ten Booms knew many people in Haarlem, and with the Lord's leading, they were able to enlist the help of many. One man was able to secure ration cards for the Jews; another man working with the phone company reconnected the Beje's phone. An electrical warning system was installed. Willem helped make contacts with people who lived in the countryside of Holland. Farms and homes away from the cities made the safest hiding places.

To protect the true identities of the people involved in the underground, all the workers went by the name Smit. When Kik took his Tante Corrie to a meeting of the national Dutch underground, Corrie met a Mr. Smit who would play a very important role in the operation on the Barteljorisstraat. This Mr. Smit would supervise the building of a secret room in the Beje.

Corrie organized the underground operation.

Mr. Smit arrived at the Beje and inspected the odd, old building.

"This is a marriage made in heaven!" he declared, referring to the two buildings that made up the Beje. He climbed the twisting stair well to the third floor of the smaller building and inspected Corrie's bedroom.

"Take a good look at your room, Miss ten Boom. In one week you won't believe your eyes!"

The days that followed were busy ones at the Beje. At all hours of the day or night, men showed up at the door to work on the secret room. They used bricks to build the new wall, all of which had to be brought in a few at a time for safety's sake. Under Mr. Smit's direction, the brick wall was plastered and painted. He super vised the construction of a bookshelf that ran the length of the new wall.

Finally the secret room was finished.

The secret room

"What do you think?" Mr. Smit asked them. Corrie, Betsie, and Casper stared in astonishment at the room. It looked almost exactly as it had before, except for the bookshelves, but the bookshelves were obviously as old as the house!

Corrie peered at the new-old wall, vainly looking for a clue to where the entrance to the secret room was located. "I give up," she said to Mr. Smit. "Where is it?"

Mr. Smit laughed with pleasure as he kneeled down in front of the bookcase. He reached over to the lefthand corner at the bottom of the shelf and lifted up a two-foot square panel. "This is the gateway to safety."

"Superb job, Mr. Smit." A familiar voice sounded behind Corrie, and she turned to greet her brother.

"Willem, isn't this incredible?"

He lifted up the panel.

"It certainly is, Corrie." He shook hands with Mr. Smit and together they walked down the stairs. The family gathered in the dining room while Betsie made a pot of tea.

Finished with his tea, Mr. Smit rose from his chair and bade the ten Booms good-bye. Willem and Corrie walked him to the door and thanked him for his help.

"This job of saving lives is the best job I have ever had," he said softly.

Corrie watched him leave, then turned to her brother with a question. "Who is that man?"

"He's an architect," Willem replied. "Perhaps one of the best known in all of Europe."

"What's his name?" Corrie asked without thinking.

Willem looked at his sister and smiled, "Smit."

"He's one of the best known architects in Europe."

More and more Jews made their way to the refuge on the Barteljorisstraat; more and more were safely hidden away by the underground. In 1943, January's breath blew fiercely cold upon Holland and took its toll on the Dutch people. There was very little coal or wood available for burning, and some resorted to chopping down the trees in Haarlem for firewood. The winter dragged on, and hiding places in the country became scarce. It became clear that it would be necessary to use secret locations within the city.

By the summer of 1943, six refugees (four men and three women) found a permanent hiding place in the Beje itself. Betsie planned activities and mini-concerts in the evening to help ease the boredom and fear of the fugitives. Together they became a close-knit family. Casper and his daughters did all they could to make their new friends feel at home in the Beje.

The winter took its toll.

As the underground work increased, the ris[k]
increased as well. Corrie knew they were bein[g]
watched, and once a neighbor warned her that th[e]
refugees living at the Beje were being too noisy
With Kik's help, they conducted drills with th[e]
warning buzzers until everyone could get to th[e]
secret room in under two minutes. Corrie knew [it]
was only a matter of time before the Gastap[o]
came down on them.

On February 28, 1944, a stranger appeared a[t]
the Beje asking for help for his Jewish wife. H[e]
needed money to get her out of town. Corrie ar[-]
ranged for him to receive the money that after[-]
noon. After he left, Corrie headed for the stair[s.]
She wasn't feeling too well.

"Why Corrie, you've got a fever!" Betsie ex[-]
claimed, placing her hand on her sister's flushe[d]
face. "You must go to bed at once. I can tell b[y]
looking at you that you have the flu!"

"I can tell by the way I feel," Corrie mumble[d.]
She fell into her bed with relief. Betsie pulled th[e]
covers over her and in an instant she was aslee[p.]

"I need money for my wife."

Something jerked Corrie awake. It was the sound of the warning buzzer. In a blur, people raced through her door and into the secret room, disappearing behind the wall. Corrie's heart fluttered wildly as she realized it was not a drill. The Nazis were at the Beje. The underground had been betrayed.

"Oh, no," she moaned. "That man in the shop this morning!"

Seconds later the Nazis burst into Corrie's room.

"Where are you hiding them?"

"Hiding who? I don't know what you're talking about," Corrie said.

"Where is the secret room?" The Nazi yanked her to her feet.

"I don't know what you're talking about." Corrie's voice shook as she tried to dress herself as quickly as possible. All was quiet behind the wall.

"The captain will take care of you," he hissed as he shoved Corrie to the stairs. "He'll find out just what it is you don't know!"

In a blur, people raced into the secret room.

THE LIFE OF CORRIE TEN BOOM

The Nazi agent prodded her back with the nuzzle of his revolver and took her down to the shop where the captain was waiting. Corrie's body ached, and the fever wrapped itself around her. The soldier left her with the captain. His eyes narrowed as he stared at Corrie. The ticking of the clocks hammered against Corrie's pounding head as she struggled to remain standing.

"So, you are the head of this little group eh?" His voice cut sharply through the air. "Where is the secret room?"

"I don't know what you mean," she replied.

The captain slapped her face and Corrie fell against the wall.

"Where are you hiding the Jews?"

"I don't know what you mean," she stammered.

The man began to beat her, and Corrie cried out to the Lord. At the name of Jesus, the man became enraged, but he stopped beating her.

He dragged her out of the shop and up to the dining room. Casper, Betsie, and Toos were there, and Corrie collapsed into a chair next to Betsie.

*He stopped beating her
when he heard the name Jesus.*

"Well, captain?" the commander asked.

"She refuses to cooperate," he growled.

The commander pointed to Betsie. "See what you can do with her."

"Oh God, not Betsie!" Corrie moaned to herself. She looked at her father and his blue eyes held her gaze for a moment. There was a strength in his eyes that calmed Corrie while the nightmare raged around her.

The captain returned in disgust with a bruised but silent Betsie.

The walls of the Beje shook as soldiers searched for the secret room. Silently, the four seated in the chairs prayed for the hidden Jews. Heavy footsteps echoed in the stairwell and the search team approached their commander.

"We've torn the place apart, sir. Their secret room must be invisible."

The commander grunted with disgust. "Never mind. We'll keep watch on the house until those Jews starve to death." His eyes glinted with satisfaction.

"Their secret room must be invisible."

He's a madman, Corrie thought as she stared at the commander's face.

"Take them to the police station at once, along with the others."

"Others?" Corrie wondered as she looked around the dining room. "What others?"

The door to the parlor opened abruptly and the stairwell creaked with footsteps as people descended the stairs. The soldiers directed everyone out the front door. Corrie gasped with horror as she saw Willem, Nollie, and Peter pass through the door to the shop. Casper, Betsie, Toos, and Corrie followed behind the rest of the group.

The winter sun blinded Corrie's eyes as she walked down the Barteljorisstraat to the police station. She held Casper's arm, and her mind filled with memories of the countless walks she had taken with her father. Haarlem's "Grand Old Man" dearly loved to walk its streets, but this was one walk Corrie wished her father would not have to take.

"Take them to the police station."

" The dream! "

CHAPTER 8

After having their names processed at the station, they were all herded back outside to a waiting bus. Corrie, her family, and fellow workers boarded the bus. As the bus began to move, Corrie pressed her face against the glass. "I don't know where we're going, Lord, but I know You do. Keep us in Your care."

Suddenly she remembered the vision she had the first night the Germans had attacked Holland.

Corrie leaned over toward Betsie. "The dream!" she whispered.

Betsie nodded her head.

"He knows, Corrie," she whispered. "He goes before us."

The bus arrived at Nazi headquarters, where the prisoners were questioned for hours. Then they were ordered into a large truck. The ten Booms huddled together as best they could, with Betsie and Corrie sitting on either side of their father. As the truck made its way along the dark roads, Corrie felt her head spinning with fever. Where were they

going? What was going to happen next? The questions swirled in her brain while she wrestled with the
chilling arms of fear.

The truck rumbled to a stop in front of the fed-
eral prison at Scheveningen. It pulled into the prison
yard and the new captives were thrust into a large
room with dusty yellow walls.

The female prisoners were ordered to leave the
room.

Corrie, Betsie, Nollie, Toos, and the other
women turned from their places along the wall and
followed the matron across the floor to a forbidding
steel door. As Corrie walked past her Father, her
stomach knotted with the desire to run to him and
hold him, to protect him from the horrors of prison.

"The Lord be with you, Father!"

"And also with you, my children." His face
radiated the peace of Christ. "The best is yet to be."

With a quick slam of the door, Corrie lost sight of
her father. She would never see him again.

The voice of a male guard shot across the room
and jerked the women to attention. "The rest of
you follow me."

Corrie lost sight of her father.

THE LIFE OF CORRIE TEN BOOM

One by one, the new women prisoners wer put in their cells. Corrie watched as Nollie, Bet sie, and Toos were shoved into different cells Corrie was put into a cell number 384, alone an delirious with fever.

She fell onto the cot in the corner of her ce and the fever took control of her. The evening stalked silently into the prison and underline Corrie's loneliness in the solitary cell. No longe able to control her thoughts, memories swarme around her and punished her already broke heart.

Nollie stood at the side of her cot.

"Don't you like my hat, Corrie? Do you thin Tante Jans will let me wear it to school? She' probably say it's sinful!" Nollie giggled an turned away. Corrie reached out for her bu grasped only air.

"Must be hallucinating," she panted, struggl ing to sit up. "Mustn't think about home."

"Mustn't think about home."

"Corrie, my dear, do you think you could take a look at this watch? It's quite a difficult piece but I know you can do it." Father ten Boom held the watch out to Corrie and she strained to take it from him.

"I know you can do it, my dear!" He smiled at her, holding out the watch.

"Can't reach it, Pappa," she moaned. "Can't reach it."

"You are such a shrimp, Corrie!" Willem's young voice chimed in. "I'll race you to the canal!"

"Wait for me, Will!" Corrie called out to her brother.

"Silence!" A cold voice from behind the cell door cut through Corrie's feverish imaginings and for a moment slapped her back into reality. "Solitary prisoners will remain silent!"

Corrie lay back down and in the silence that followed, tears flowed quietly down her cheeks. She wept until the dirty mattress was wet with her sorrow.

"Solitary prisoners will remain silent."

"I can't do it, Lord," she cried. "It's too much for me. I just can't."

When tears would no longer come, Corrie turned on her side and cupped her hands over her face. Empty of tears, she felt engulfed in the emptiness of her lonely cell. Then thoughts of home returned to penetrate the blackness, but this time they came on the wings of calmness and comfort. As Corrie felt her own hands on her face, she remembered how her father would tuck his children into bed each night. The last thing he would do was touch each child gently on the face, as if to say "I love you and I'm watching over you."

The memory pushed aside the emptiness in her cell and Corrie reached out for her heavenly Father. "Cover me, Lord," she prayed. "Hide me under the shelter of Your wings."

She fell asleep with His words on her lips.

The days at Scheveningen passed slowly, but Corrie sensed the Presence of the Lord with her.

"Hide me under Your wings."

She recovered from her illness, and as each day ended, she marked it down on the walls of her cell.

Sometimes, the loneliness and sheer boredom of her confinement loomed larger than life and threatened to sweep her into mindlessness. At times she felt like a tiny dot on a black line that stretched on forever. But those were just feelings, she reminded herself. We must walk by faith.

Whenever it was possible, the prisoners communicated with one another by shouting through the openings on the doors. To Corrie's amazement and joy, she learned that almost everyone had been released from prison except for Betsie, Corrie, and Casper. She painfully wondered how her father was doing; she knew prison life would be too hard for an eighty-four-year-old man.

One day in April, the trap door on her cell door clanked open and in flew a letter. Corrie sat

We must walk by faith.

rooted on the cot for a few minutes, not believing what she was seeing. Finally, she picked it up. The return address was Nollie's.

Ripping open the letter, Corrie read it through a blur of tears. It was her first contact with home, and the "Dear Corrie" washed over her in a wave of love. There was good news: Everyone was free except for Corrie and Betsie. Father was free, too, but his freedom was in walking with Jesus face-to-face. He lived only nine days after his arrest.

"I know this is hard news for you to bear," the letter continued, "but try and remember what Father always used to say — 'The best is yet to be.' "

In May, Corrie was interrogated for four days by a Nazi lieutenant named Rahms. When asked who was involved in the underground, Corrie could only reply with the name "Smit." Instead

Father was truly free.

of supplying him with information, she boldly witnessed to him about Christ.

On the fourth and final day of her hearings, the Lieutenant brought out several papers and handed them to Corrie.

"What can you tell me about these papers?"

Corrie stared at the papers and recognized them immediately. The Gestapo must have found them in the Beje. There were lists of names, addresses, and specific details about the underground work. Corrie knew she was staring at her own death penalty.

"I can't explain them, sir." Corrie's mind reeled with the thought that not only did those papers condemn her, they also condemned many of the people who worked with the underground.

The lieutenant took the papers from Corrie and walked toward the woodburning stove in his office. To Corrie's utmost surprise, he opened the door of the stove and shoved the papers in.

Corrie was staring at her own death penalty.

Through silent tears of joy, Corrie watched the bright yellow flames devour the evidence.

Several days later, Corrie was summoned to the lieutenant's office again. Once inside his office, Corrie found herself surrounded by her family. She stared at them, not daring to believe they were actually there.

"It is my imagination. I am only dreaming," she whispered.

"No, no, Corrie dear. We really are here!"

She looked up into Willem's eyes and collapsed in his arms. Nollie, Betsie, Flip, and Tine gathered around her and mingled their tears with her own. Corrie looked at each face and marveled at God's grace.

"You look wonderful!" Nollie hugged Corrie again and slipped something into Corrie's pocket. It was a tiny Bible.

"I will do all I can to get you and Betsie released," Lieutenant Rahms said quietly, "but I must warn you that it is a next-to-impossible task."

"I am only dreaming."

Betsie and Corrie tearfully enjoyed the precious minutes with their family and then reluctantly said good-bye. Corrie was overjoyed with the treasure in her pocket — the Bible. She prayed a prayer of heartfelt thanks to the Shepherd who was so lovingly taking care of her. He had sent her His Word to keep her and comfort her in those long, lonely days of solitary confinement. Little did she know that her little Bible would become a source of light not only for herself, but for countless other women as well.

In June, all prisoners at Scheveningen were transferred by train to Vught concentration camp in Holland.

There was treasure in her pocket.

I am in a slave market.

CHAPTER 9

In Barracks #4 of Vught concentration camp, Betsie held Corrie's hand tightly.

"We are together, Corrie! I don't know what lies ahead, but we are together!" Corrie squeezed Betsie's hand in agreement. Together they would face whatever would come.

A stern-faced female guard marched into the barracks.

"Roll call is at 5:00 A.M. and 6:00 P.M. If anyone is late, roll call will be earlier. Today you will be assigned to work details." She turned to leave and then stopped for a moment. "The disobedient will pay for their disobedience."

The room was silent after she left. A guard ordered the prisoners to assemble in ranks of five in the main yard. Several officers walked up and down the rows of women, checking their lists and studying the women. The June sun felt warm on Corrie's face, and she squinted in the brightness. As the men consulted one another, a strange feeling swept over Corrie. *A slave market. I am in a slave market, waiting to be sold.*

Eventually they called Corrie's name and assigned her to work in the Phillips Factory where they assembled radios for German fighter planes. Mr. Moorman, the *Oberkapo* (prisoner in charge of a work detail), was a kind man who gave them a tour of the factory and explained what to do. Then he took Corrie to her bench.

"We must keep production up, or there will be trouble. However, they can't tell the difference between a good radio and a faulty one, so don't worry if you happen to connect the wrong wires." He looked at Corrie to see if she understood.

She smiled up at him. "I will do my best."

The workday at Vught was twelve hours long. When Corrie returned to the barracks, she found Betsie waiting at the door for her with bandaged hands.

"Betsie, what in the world happened?"

In the factory, they assembled radios.

"They assigned me to the rope detail. You have to braid the ropes together." Betsie sighed and looked down at her hands. "The rope is very course, and I burned my hands raw on them."

Seeing the look of concern on Corrie's face, Betsie stopped and lay a bandaged hand on her sister's shoulder. "It's all right, Corrie. They've given me a new assignment. I am to stay right here in the barracks and sew prison uniforms with the other old ladies." She laughed. "That's what they called me, an old lady!"

The days at Vught passed quickly. The work was hard and the lack of food took its toll on the prisoners. Betsie especially suffered from hunger, and her weight went down to ninety-six pounds. Every day Corrie brought a portion of her lunch back to the barracks for Betsie. In the evenings, they read the Bible to all who would listen and shared the message of God's overwhelming love.

Food was scarce.

Roll calls were long, boring and exhausting, and when the prisoners' performances were less than perfect, roll call was used as punishment. To stand at attention for an hour at a time racked the body with pain, but for Betsie and Corrie, roll call became an opportunity to see the wonder of creation. The August sun would go down with all the majesty of a royal procession. The reds and golds lit up the sky and scattered their brilliance over the yard of the camp, engulfing the prisoners in color. In the glow of those moments, Corrie and Betsie knew God was displaying a picture of His Presence. It was a piece of glory, a reminder of God's kingdom that never fails. They felt every bit of pain as their muscles cried out for rest, but the display of their Lord's power ignited their hope in Him.

The men's camp at Vught was separated from the women's by a wall of barbed wire. During the lunch break at the factory, women would gather

Roll calls were tedious.

at the fence and try to get information abou
husbands and sons who were there. Others wer
fortunate enough to be working in the factories sid
by side with their loved ones. But happiness i
Vught was a fragile thing; often a wife would wait i
vain for her husband to join her for the day. Daily
the piercing sound of gunshots in the men's cam
grimly announced the death of more prisoners.

In September, the sound of bombs exploding i
the distance kindled hope among the prisoner
that the Allies were in Holland. Maybe freedom
was around the corner! Maybe the Germans wer
retreating! At the factory, Mr. Moorman ex
plained that what they were hearing was actuall
the Germans destroying bridges. The Allies wer
coming, but they weren't in Holland yet.

All the women were ordered to return to thei
barracks.

In the men's camp, soldiers lined hundreds o
prisoners up against the back wall and systemati
cally shot them in the head.

The sound of gun shots filled the air.

The next morning, the women and the surviving male prisoners were herded out of the camp. Corrie and Betsie marched together, their precious Bible hidden in Corrie's prison uniform. They arrived at the train tracks and were ordered to stand at attention. A freight train was waiting for its living cargo, the windowless boxcars forming a dreary line on the tracks. At a signal from the commander, the prisoners were ordered to climb into the boxcars. Soldiers pushed and prodded the people like cattle, until each car was stuffed with between eighty and one hundred prisoners.

The train jolted to a start several hours after it had been loaded. The stench in the boxcars became unbearable and the darkness overwhelming. Their destination was Germany. Slowly the engine pulled the living nightmare down the tracks for four days and four nights. It seemed to Corrie that the prince of hell himself must have masterminded this horrible exodus. She wondered if they would survive the trip. The train stopped and

People were shoved into the train.

started several times, as if to prolong the agony. Finally, on the fourth day, it came to a full stop.

The doors were pulled open and the light of day blinded the prisoners as they poured out of the boxcars. Corrie squinted her eyes and saw a small lake near a grove of pine trees. In the distance there was a small town. A squad of soldiers directed the prisoners onto a road and ordered them to march. The lake borrowed its sparkle from the sun and shimmered in the morning light, unaware of the line of human misery that stumbled past its shores. One mile later, they arrived at Ravensbruck, the only all-women's concentration camp of Hitler's regime. Some women began to weep; Corrie looked over at her sister. Betsie grasped Corrie's hand and whispered the word "together." Together they walked on, clinging to the knowledge that they were not alone; their Savior walked with them through the gates of Ravensbruck.

They arrived at Ravensbruck.

For three days the prisoners stood at attention in the camp's yard. At night, they slept on the ground. At the end of the third day, S.S. guards escorted the prisoners to the receiving building of the camp. Corrie panicked as she watched the women put all their belongings on the tables and take off their clothes to enter a large shower room. It would take a miracle to get the Bible past the S.S. guards. Corrie whispered a prayer.

"Corrie," Betsie groaned. "I . . . terrible cramps. . . ."

Quickly grabbing Betsie before she could fall, Corrie asked a guard where the bathrooms were located.

"Bathrooms?" he said scornfully. "What bathrooms? Use the shower room!" He led them to the shower room and left them there alone. Corrie looked around the room and saw the answer to her prayer. There was a stack of old furniture in the room. She pulled the Bible out from under her uniform and hit it behind the furniture.

Corrie saw the answer to her prayer.

They returned to the main room, undressed and marched past the S.S. guards to the shower room. The water was cold, but it felt good as it washed away the dirt of many days. Corrie drew two prison dresses from a pile and gave one to Betsie. The dresses were worn thin, and when Corrie stuffed the Bible under her uniform, she knew it was hopeless. There was no human way she could conceal her secret from the guards.

"Lord, please hide me behind your angels," she prayed desperately.

The women reentered the main room and Corrie watched as the S.S. guards searched each woman thoroughly, frisking them one by one. When it was Corrie's turn, she walked right past the guards. They did not even glance at her! Corrie's heart sang. *Aufseherinnen* (S.S. women) conducting a second round of searches pushed Corrie along past the second inspection. The Bible was safe!

The newcomers were sent to the quarantine

Corrie walked past the guards.

block, where Corrie and Betsie were assigned to Barracks #8. They squeezed into a bed with three other women and fell asleep.

At 4:00 A.M., a whistle blew and awakened the prisoners for their morning ration of food. At 4:30, they assembled on the Lagerstrasse, the broad street that ran the length of the camp. The women were organized in groups of one hundred each, ten women per row. At roll call, the guards counted the prisoners, checking and rechecking until the numbers coincided with the camp's official list. If anyone was missing, the others remained at attention until the missing were found. Latecomers were beaten without mercy.

Directly across from the quarantine barracks on the Lagerstrasse was the Strafblock. This was the punishment section of the barracks. The normal punishment was twenty-five lashes with a stick, but sometimes prisoners were sentenced to fifty to seventy-five blows. Day and night, screams of terror and utter despair filtered through the walls of the Strafblock.

**Screams of terror
from the Strafblock filled the air.**

In between roll calls, the new prisoners were ordered to their barracks. Corrie pulled out the Bible and Betsie began to read to all who would listen. Each day the number of women who gathered together increased. Love was searching for His children, and Corrie and Betsie held out His message to the condemned women of Ravensbruck. As the realities of the concentration camp worsened, the reality of God's Presence became clearer and brighter.

In the middle of October the new prisoners were transferred to permanent barracks. At the last row of buildings, at Barracks #28, the guard called out Prisoner 66729 and Prisoner 66730. Corrie and Betsie marched into the new quarters.

In the front part of the barrack was a large room with tables and benches where women sat knitting gray army socks. There were two rooms off the main room where the prisoners slept. A prison worker took Corrie and Betsie into their assigned room.

"This room was built to accommodate two hundred women," said the worker, "but there are seven hundred living here now. Not to mention the millions

Seven hundred women lived in one room.

of fleas," she added. Corrie groaned, but Betsie said, "Praise the Lord."

The large room was filled with wooden platforms three levels high. The platforms were grouped tightly together with only a few narrow aisles making a way to get through the room. Corrie and Betsie's bunk was on the second tier in the middle of an island of platforms. They had to climb up and crawl over several bunks to get to their own.

At six o'clock the whistle sounded for the evening roll call and Betsie and Corrie made their way to the Lagerstrasse. They took their places with the other women of Barracks #28. The newcomers couldn't take their eyes off the women of Ravensbruck who stood around them. Their bodies were wasted away, their skin deformed with running sores. But the thing that scared Corrie the most was the look on their faces — they stared straight ahead, their eyes glazed over with despair. Death was written on their faces.

"Help us to bring them Your hope," Corrie prayed silently.

Death was written on their faces.

The women worked eleven hours a day.

CHAPTER 10

The following day, after roll call, the prisoners were assigned to their work details. A nearby factory paid the Nazis for laborers and every day thousands of women marched to the factory and reported for work. Corrie's and Betsie's first assignment was with the Sieman's factory. Located south of the camp next to the railroad tracks, the plant's work consisted of dragging heavy pieces of metal from railroad cars to the factory building. After eleven hours of exhausting labor, the women marched back to the camp, engulfed once again by the gray concrete walls of Ravensbruck.

In the evening, the ten Boom sisters started their Bible studies in Barracks #28. Women gathered around one of the few lights in the huge room — women from all over Europe and of all denominations. They would sing quietly and then the Bible would be read. Corrie breathed a prayer of thanks that her father had taught them German. Many of the women understood German and for those who did not, others would translate the reading for them. Each night more women joined the group.

"I can't understand why the guards never come in here," Corrie said to Betsie one evening as they climbed over the bunks to go to bed. "Not once have they come in to inspect the place. It's amazing." Corrie settled down in the straw and scratched one of her countless flea bites.

"I know why they don't come in here," Betsie replied. Corrie could tell by the tone of Betsie's voice that she was smiling in the drakness. "I discovered the reason today. The guards refuse to come in because of the fleas!" Betsie laughed. "Fleas, Cornelia ten Boom. Because of the fleas, we can freely share the gospel with our fellow prisoners."

In November Corrie and Betsie's work assignment was changed: They now worked within the camp, digging up uneven patches of ground and smoothing them out with huge metal rollers. The digging took its toll on Betsie. Each day she weakened, until she could hardly carry her shovel.

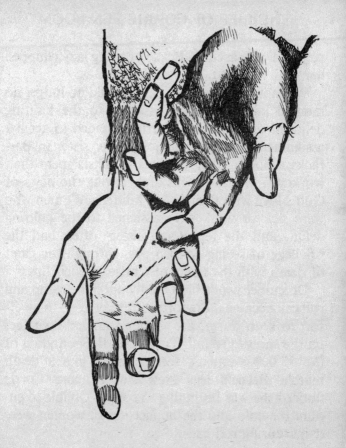

"Praise the Lord for fleas!"

A guard who accused Betsie of being lazy whipped her until she bled.

When it was clear that Betsie could no longer do manual labor, she was assigned to the knitting detail in the barracks. Corrie managed to get her assignment changed and joined her sister in Barracks #28. Together Corrie and Betsie spent their workdays knitting socks and sharing the news of God's love with their fellow knitters. Women who were sick or weak were assigned to the knitting detail, and the ten Boom sisters often had the privilege of seeing women pass through the gates of death with the name of Christ on their lips.

December winds blew coldly upon the camp and roll call became more torturous than ever. In an effort to keep warm, the women stamped their feet on the snowy ground. To Corrie, the pounding of the 37,000 women's feet sounded like a death march. Betsie's legs grew weaker, and Corrie noticed she was beginning to cough. Unable to endure the cold and the hunger, some women were dying during roll call.

The women stamped their feet.

One night in the barracks, Betsie had something important to tell Corrie. Corrie studied Betsie's thin face. Her cheeks were sunken and there were dark circles under her eyes.

"What is it, Betsie?"

"The Lord has shown me what we are to do after we get out of here."

"You mean we will be released? Are you sure?"

"Oh, yes, it is quite clear. We will have a house in Holland for rehabilitation. People who have suffered in the concentration camps will need to recover before they can again have normal lives.

"The house is very large — a mansion really — with lots of windows and shiny wood floors. There's a large yard with many gardens where the people can grow flowers and vegetables."

"When, Betsie? When will this happen?"

"We will be free before the new year comes.

"And what a staircase! It's such a marvelous, wide staircase. And there are statues, you know, in the front hall."

Corrie studied Betsie's emaciated face.

"And after the war," Betsie continued, "We are going to have a concentration camp."

"What?" Corrie said loudly. She sat up and bumped her head on the bunk above her.

"Shhh. You'll wake everybody up. The camp is in Germany. They need so desperately to learn how to love."

Corrie lay back down and thought about the *Aufseherinnen* and the S.S. men.

"Only God could teach them how to love," she muttered.

"We must tell them. We must tell everyone that no pit is so deep that God is not deeper still." Her voice grew weaker. "And we must paint the camp with bright colors and plant flowers."

The next morning when the whistle blew for roll call, Betsie could not move. She was carried to the camp hospital where she died.

Corrie doubled over, sobbing. "It can't be," she wept. "It can't be!"

Corrie began to walk around the camp in a daze, stumbling on the snowy streets. She heard footsteps running, and someone grabbed her from behind.

Corrie walked around the camp in a daze.

It was Mien. "You've got to come."

"I don't want to see her. I know she's dead."

"You've got to see her, Corrie. I know a way to get in without anyone seeing us. Come on."

Mien took her to a window in the back of the hospital.

"They put the bodies in the washroom." She lifted up the window. "Climb in."

Corrie hesitated, but Mein insisted she go in. She lowered herself into the room and covered her eyes with her hands. A line of starved bodies lay on the floor.

"Look, Corrie! Look at her!"

Corrie looked down at Betsie, expecting to see her thin sister. What she did see took her breath away. Betsie was beautiful. Every trace of suffering had disappeared; her face was full and clear, as if she had never been starved or ill.

"It's a miracle," Mien whispered.

Corrie nodded wordlessly as she stared at her sister.

Betsie was free.

Betsie was free.

A few days later, Prisoner 66730 was called out of her line.

"Stand at the head of the line."

Other women were ordered to join Corrie, and they waited for roll call to end. The wind was especially cold that day and Corrie felt her legs and feet begin to swell. She could see the smoke from the cremation ovens rise above the camp. Perhaps it was her turn to die.

Corrie shuddered in the cold and committed herself to the Lord. Roll call continued for three hours, and Corrie used that time to tell a young girl next to her about Christ. The girl listened carefully and then asked the Savior to come into her life.

Finally, roll call ended and Corrie was ordered to report to the administration offices. An officer called her name and handed Corrie a piece of paper. She stared down at it, afraid to believe what she was seeing. It was a certificate of discharge! She was not going to die, after all. She was going to live!

She stared at the paper.

Corrie shuffled from one desk to the next one. Another officer gave her a pass for the train, then she was directed to a room where medical inspections were taking place. Sharp pains shot up and down her legs and ankles as she waited in the line. The doctor took one look at her legs and ordered her to the hospital.

"They'll let you out if the swelling goes down."

Corrie stayed in the hospital for seven days. The days passed slowly and were filled with horror as Corrie witnessed the cruelty of the nurses there. Many of the women were dying, begging for water, but the nurses would only laugh and make fun of them. Some prisoners fell out of their beds, unable to move, and were left on the floor to die.

On the seventh day, Corrie passed the physical and was given civilian clothes and a coat, then ordered to put her signature on a paper that stated she had never been ill-treated at Ravensbruck. She signed the useless piece of paper.

"Report to the gate," an S.S. man snarled.

The nurses made fun of the prisoners.

As Corrie waited at the gate with a small group of women, someone from Barracks #28 approached her.

"Corrie," she whispered, "that girl you witnessed to at your last roll call died today. She spoke to me about you. I thought you would want to know."

The girl scurried away at the sound of a soldier's boots. The guard pushed open the iron gates and an *Aufseherin* gave the command to follow. Corrie felt she was dreaming as she passed through the gates. She saw the lake, pine trees still gracing its shores. The steeple of a church in the nearby town was pointing to heaven. Heaven, Pappa was there, and Betsie, and many other women who had been introduced to Christ at Ravensbruck. Corrie breathed a prayer of thanks. She had left her Bible with one of the women, and she hoped that many more would find eternal life in its pages.

The guard pushed open the iron gates.

THE LIFE OF CORRIE TEN BOOM

The *Aufseherin* led the ex-prisoners to the train station and left them there. It seemed odd to Corrie that she was free and the *Aufseherin* was returning to prison. Corrie reached Berlin on New Year's Day. One week later, at Ravensbruck, all women in Corrie's age group were killed. Corrie had been released by mistake.

At the huge train station at Berlin, Corrie boarded the train headed for Holland. After three days of traveling, the train crossed the border of her homeland and pulled into the station at Groningen. Corrie made her way to the hospital there. She was exhausted and her legs ached. She hadn't eaten since she left Ravensbruck. Once she was inside the hospital, the nurses fed her, made up a bed for her, then led her to a room with a white tub filled with clean, warm water.

The nurse closed the door behind her and Corrie lowered herself into the tub. Her ravaged skin welcomed the healing warmth of the water, and Corrie cried for joy. She was free. She was really free.

She was free.

Something had changed.

CHAPTER 11

Ten days later, Corrie was at Hilversum, weeping in her brother's arms. Tine hovered around her like a mother hen and insisted that she stay at least two weeks with them. In the days that followed, Corrie told them about Ravensbruck, about Betsie's shining life the miracle at her death. Willem told Corrie the news about Kik, who had been arrested and sent to Germany. They did not know if he was dead or alive.

Corrie wanted to go home to the Beje. Willem arranged the trip and a friend drove her to Haarlem.

But something had changed. Corrie had learned that God alone was her home. As much as she loved the Beje, she knew she couldn't stay. Betsie often said the safest place to be was in the center of God's will, and Corrie knew what His will for her was. She must tell everyone she could that no darkness can overcome the light of God's love.

THE LIFE OF CORRIE TEN BOOM

Early in May, 1945, Holland was liberated b
the Allies, and the country rejoiced in it
freedom. Corrie went from church to church an
home to home, sharing with people what she an
Betsie had learned in Ravensbruck. After on
meeting, a woman offered her home to Corri
for the rehabilitation work Betsie had spoken o
in Ravensbruck.

Corrie accompanied the woman to her home
and as she looked up at the large windows an
the surrounding gardens, she could almost hea
Betsie's voice. "It's a mansion, really. . . ." He
shoes squeaked on the shiny wood floors, an
she studied the statues set into the walls, tryin
not to cry as she climbed the grand staircase.

The Lord opened doors for Corrie all ove
Europe, and she faithfully carried the message o
His love to all who would listen. Often, sh
would lay a map out on her bed and ask the Lor

She climbed the grand staircase.

where He wanted her to go next. Sensitive to the Spirit's leading, she would go where He said to go.

She made her first trip to America where for almost a year she proclaimed the gospel. She preached the gospel wherever she could, but she especially enjoyed going to the prisons to share her story. From Sing Sing to San Quentin, Corrie spoke of the power of God's love. Sometimes before she began to speak, the prisoners would disrupt the meeting with jeers and yells. What did that old lady have to say to them? Then Corrie would begin talking about her prison term and everyone would become quiet. She had been where they were now. She knew how they felt and she gave them the key to inner freedom — Jesus Christ.

As her time in America came to an end, Corrie knew in her heart that the Lord was ready to send

Corrie ministered in prisons.

her to a place she did not want to go: Germany. *Surely I have suffered enough, Lord,* she thought. *Don't send me back to that terrible place.* But the Lord insisted, and Corrie submitted to His will.

Corrie arrived in Germany and was overwhelmed by the needs that stretched out before her. Millions of Germans were homeless, millions were in despair over the evils wrought by Adolf Hitler. People had set up homes wherever they could; Corrie discovered a factory crowded with people. She decided she would live with them and try to reach them for the Lord. The living conditions were crowded and the air laced with horrible smells, but Corrie was used to that. She lived out her faith among the people and pointed them to Christ.

While in Germany, Corrie began to see more of Betsie's vision come to pass. A man from a

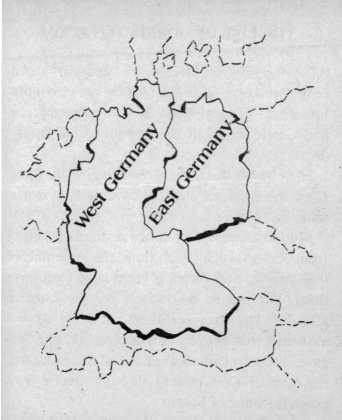

Corrie returned to Germany.

relief organization offered her the use of a concentration camp in Darmstadt for her rehabilitation work. The gray barracks were painted green, and Corrie smiled at the thought of her sister's dream.

How wonderful to be in the hands of the living God, she thought. *It is the adventure of a lifetime.*

More than once, Corrie saw a guard or a nurse from Ravensbruck. Each time, she remembered their cruelty and found it impossible to forgive them. She prayed desperately for the Lord to give her His love for them, and He always answered that prayer. In His strength, she forgave, and as she shook the hand of one ex-guard, the love of God poured through Corrie in a powerful wave of love.

Corrie followed Her Lord wherever He led her.

She shook the guard's hand.

THE LIFE OF CORRIE TEN BOOM

She traveled to over sixty countries and preached to all kinds of people from all walks of life. She told the story of surviving Ravensbruck, where over 95,000 women lost their lives. Corrie's release was no mistake; it was the hand of her Lord directing her path and unveiling His plan. She learned that when all seems lost, Jesus remains, and the best is yet to be.

In her travels, Corrie discovered that the needs of man are the same all over. All people need the Savior, and many are ignorant of His love and how well He provides for His people. As she observed the empty hearts of men and women, she was reminded of a little boy in her Bible class for retarded children. Corrie was telling the class about the feeding of the five thousand, and little Carl was totally engrossed in the story. Suddenly, he leaped out of his seat, crying out enthusiastically: "There is plenty! There is plenty! Take as much as you want!"

Corrie wished people could see God's love and care for them as clearly as Carl did.

Corrie traveled to over sixty countries.

THE LIFE OF CORRIE TEN BOOM

Corrie told the story of the war years in her book *The Hiding Place*. It became a bestseller, and World Wide Pictures made a film based on Corrie's book. One day while the film was being made, Corrie watched as the woman who played her came through the gates of Ravensbruck. The impact of her suffering swept over Corrie; she remembered the pain, the loss of her sister and her father. She wept openly, and as she wept, the Lord healed Corrie's deep hurt. She realized her suffering had paved the way for her to preach the good news: There is no pit so deep that God is not deeper still.

Corrie ten Boom continued to serve the Lord well into her eighties. In 1977, Corrie settled in California in a home she named "Shalom House." She was no longer able to travel all over the world as she had been doing for so many years; her heart was weakening. But despite the

She watched herself walk through the gate.

obstacles of a weak body, she had tremendous drive and energy that enabled her to accomplish goals she set for herself with the leading of the Lord.

Corrie was writing books and making films to bring people to know Jesus when at the age of eighty-six she suffered a stroke that paralyzed her right side and took away her ability to speak. The paralysis eventually disappeared, but she never regained the ability to speak aloud. This, however did not stop her from communicating. Her companion, Pamela Rosewell, the housekeeper, and Lotte, a close friend of Corrie's, managed to understand Corrie's desires and thoughts by asking her questions that Corrie could answer by signaling yes or no.

Lotte helped her finish another devotional book, and Corrie received visitors to Shalom House, ministering without words but with her

At the age of eighty-six,
Corrie suffered a stroke.

eyes and her smile. She enjoyed the garden in the backyard and often walked outside, enjoying the flowers and the sky. No doubt she was often reminded of her mother's and Betsie's love for flowers and the blue sky.

Corrie submitted to the Lord at this difficult time of not being able to speak freely. There were tears of frustration at times, but she never rebelled in anger against her Lord. In 1979, Corrie suffered another stroke: This one left her incapable of walking. She could sit up in a wheel chair, however, and so her tour of the garden was done by chair, with a friend pushing gently from behind. She could understand and communicate with a nod or a simple yes. It was difficult for those who loved her to see her so confined, but they marveled at Corrie's peace in the midst of such suffering.

In the fall of 1980, Corrie suffered her final stroke. She survived the stroke, but was no longer able to sit in her wheel chair. She was extremely weak and her friends could see in her eyes a deep desire to go home to be with her Lord. However, the

Corrie often walked in the garden.

days continued to stretch out before her, and once again those who cared for her were amazed at Corrie's surrender to her Father's will. For some reason, God chose to have her live for two and a half more years, silent and unable to move from her bed.

God's plans are never wasteful, but fruitful. In the past, Corrie's mother, her voice silenced and her body still because of a stroke, had managed to minister to others through the prayer in her heart and the love that shone in her eyes. Now Corrie did the same. God's love flowed through her to those who lived with her and those who came to see her at her home. People literally experienced Christ's love and Christ's Presence in Corrie. She witnessed silently to the fact that our peace, joy, and fulfillment come not from what we can do in life for God but from God Himself.

Thirty-nine years before, while in solitary confinement in Scheveningen Prison, Corrie wrote to her sister Nollie about God's timing: "Once I

God's plans are fruitful.

asked to be freed but the Lord said, 'My grace is sufficient for you.' I am continually looking at Him and trying not to be impatient. I won't be here one minute longer than God deems necessary. Pray for me that I can wait for His timing."[1]

Now Corrie patiently and joyfully waited for her freedom from the prison of her body, and when the day came, she was ready.

On her birthday, April 15, 1983, Corrie walked through the gates of her Father's heaven into His glory. No doubt there was a great celebration that day in heaven.

Corrie's path took her to many places. She always called herself a "tramp for the Lord." From a concentration camp to foreign palaces, Corrie told the eternal story of God's love for all people. Her journey ended in the unveiled Presence of her Lord face-to-face.

"The path of the righteous is like the first gleam of dawn, shining ever brighter till the full light of day."

[1] Corrie ten Boom. PRISON LETTERS (Old Tappan, New Jersey: Fleming H. Revell Company, 1975).

I am continually looking at Him.

Glossary

Allies   countries that fought against Germany, Italy and later Japan during World War II; in particular, Great Britain, the Soviet Union, and the United States.

apprentice   a person who contracted with a craftsman to work with him in order to learn his craft or trade.

Aufseherin   female S.S. guard (Aufseherinnen — plural).

Beje   home of the Ten Booms; pronounced bay-yay.

Barteljorisstraat   street in the Dutch city of Haarlem where the Beje was located.

concentration camp   a prison camp where "enemies of the state" are held captive. In Hitler's regime, concentration camps were extermination camps where millions of people were executed. Over six million Jews died in Hitler's camps.

crematory   building that housed the cremation ovens; the ovens were used to burn up the corpses of people who died or were killed in the concentration camps.

Nazi   member of the National Socialist German Workers' Party.

S.S.   from the German 'Schutzstaffel'; special police serving the Nazi party.

Strafblock   the barracks at Ravensbruck where prisoners were punished.

Bibliography

Rosewell, Pamela. THE FIVE SILENT YEARS OF CORRIE TEN BOOM. Grand Rapids: Zondervan Publishing House, 1986.

ten Boom, Corrie. AMAZING LOVE. London: Christian Literature Crusade, 1953.

ten Boom, Corrie. EACH NEW DAY. Westwood, New Jersey: Barbour and Company, Inc., 1977.

ten Boom, Corrie. FATHER TEN BOOM. Old Tappan, New Jersey: Fleming H. Revell Company.

ten Boom, Corrie with Carlson, C.C. IN MY FATHER'S HOUSE. Old Tappan, New Jersey: Fleming H. Revell Company, 1976.

ten Boom, Corrie. PRISON LETTERS. New York: Bantam Books, Inc., by arrangement with Fleming H. Revell, 1978.

ten Boom, Corrie with Sherrill, John and Elizabeth. THE HIDING PLACE. Old Tappan, New Jersey: Fleming H. Revell Company, 1971.

ten Boom, Corrie with Buckingham, Jamie. TRAMP FOR THE LORD. Fort Washington, Pennsylvania: Christian Literature Crusade and Old Tappan, New Jersey: Fleming H. Revell, 1974.

Tillion, Germaine, transl. by Satterwhite, Gerald. RAVENS-BRÜCK. Garden City, New York: Anchor Press, 1975.

© MCMLXXXIX by Barbour Publishing, Inc.

ISBN 1-55748-102-4

All rights reserved. No part of this publication may be reproduced or transmitted in any form or by any means without written permission of the publisher.

All Scripture quotations are taken from the Authorized King James Version of the Bible.

Published by Barbour Publishing, Inc.
        P.O. Box 719
        Uhrichsville, Ohio 44683
        http://www.barbourbooks.com

Member of the
Evangelical Christian
Publishers Association

Printed in the United States of America.